Australia

By Allan Fowler

Consultant
Linda Cornwell
Coordinator of School Quality and Professional Improvement
Indiana State Teachers Association

JNF 994 FOWLER

K-3

ℂℙ Children's Press®
A Division of Grolier Publishing
New York London Hong Kong Sydney
Danbury, Connecticut

Visit Children's Press® on the Internet at:
http://publishing.grolier.com

Designer: Herman Adler Design Group
Photo Researcher: Caroline Anderson
The photo on the cover shows Uluru, a well-known landform found in
Australia's outback.

Library of Congress Cataloging-in-Publication Data

Fowler, Allan.
    Australia / by Allan Fowler.
      p. cm. — (Rookie read-about geography)
    Includes index.
    Summary: An introduction to the continent of Australia, its geographical
features, people, and animals.
    ISBN 0-516-21670-8 (lib. bdg.)   0-516-27298-5 (pbk.)
    1. Australia—Juvenile literature. 2. Australia—Geography—Juvenile
literature. I. Title. II. Series.
DU96.F69   2001
994—dc21
                                00-027562

The biggest pieces of
land on Earth are called
continents. There are
seven continents.

Australia (aw-STRAYL-yuh)
is the smallest continent.

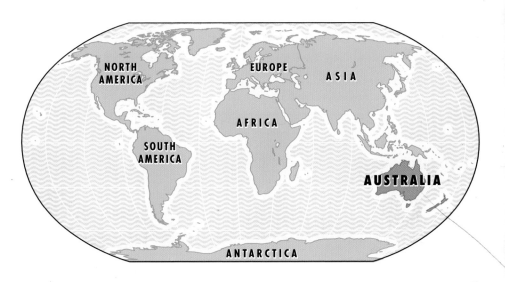

Most continents are divided into many countries. But Australia is just one country.

Australia is surrounded
by water.

You can find Australia on a globe. First, look for the equator (ee-KWAY-tur).

The equator is the imaginary line around the center of the globe.

equator

equator

You will find Australia below the equator.

Australia is often called the land "down under" because it is located under the equator.

The island of Tasmania is part of Australia. Tasmania is rainy and cool.

Mountains and waterfalls
can be found there.

Sydney (SID-nee) and
Melbourne (MEL-burn)
are Australia's biggest cities.

They are on the coast, or
edge, of the continent.

Sydney

Melbourne

There are many white-sand beaches in Australia.

People from all over the world visit these beaches to swim and lie in the sun.

The central part of
Australia is called
the "outback."

The outback is dry
and flat. Large deserts
are found there.

In the outback, there are also ranches called sheep stations. Ranchers raise sheep for wool.

Australia produces more wool than any other country.

Many people visit the
outback to see Uluru
(OO-loo-rooh).

Uluru is a huge, reddish
rock. It is one and a half
miles long and more than
one thousand feet high!

In the ocean off the coast of Australia is the Great Barrier (BARE-ee-ur) Reef.

The reef is made of coral.
Coral is the skeletons of
millions of tiny sea animals.

The Great Barrier Reef is filled with strange shapes and bright colors.

Beautiful fish swim in and out of it.

Many interesting animals live in Australia. Kangaroos carry their babies in pouches.

The platypus (PLAT-uh-puss)
has webbed feet and a bill
like a duck. Its body is
covered with fur.

Can you believe that Australia is the smallest continent?

There is so much to see and do there!

Words You Know

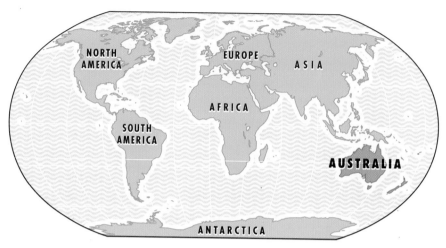

continents

globe

Great Barrier Reef

kangaroos

outback

Tasmania

Uluru

31

Index

About the Author

Allan Fowler is a freelance writer with a background in advertising. Born in New York, he now lives in Chicago and enjoys traveling.

Photo Credits

Photographs ©: Bill Bachman & Associates: 17, 31 top right; Corbis–Bettmann: 29 (Tom Brakefield); International Stock Photo: 13 (Chad Ehlers); Liaison Agency, Inc.: cover (Alain Evrard), 27 (Arne Hodalic/Saola), 11 (G. Brad Lewis), 14 (James Pozarik); Nance S. Trueworthy: 7, 8, 30 bottom left; Peter Arnold Inc.: 25 (Kelvin Aitken), 5, 10, 31 bottom left (Auscape/Ferrero), 21, 31 bottom right (Fred Bavendam), 18 (Barbara Pfeffer); Photo Researchers: 4 (WorldSat International/Science Source); Tony Stone Images: 22, 30 bottom right (Paul Chesley), 23 (William J. Hebert), 26, 31 top left (Stuart Westmorland).

Map by Bob Italiano.